T0029212

What does Grief feel like?

Korie Leigh, Ph.D.

illustrated by Mike Malbrough

free spirit
PUBLISHING®
an imprint of Teacher Created Materials

Library of Congress Cataloging-in-Publication Data
Names: Leigh, Korie, author. | Malbrough, Mike, illustrator.
Title: What does grief feel like? / Korie Leigh, Ph.D. ; illustrated by Mike Malbrough.
Description: Minneapolis, MN : Free Spirit Publishing, [2023] | Audience: Ages 3–8
Identifiers: LCCN 2022044369 (print) | LCCN 2022044370 (ebook) | ISBN 9781631987069 (hardcover) |
    ISBN 9781631987076 (ebook) | ISBN 9781631987083 (epub)
Subjects: LCSH: Grief in children—Juvenile literature. | Bereavement in children—Juvenile literature. |
    BISAC: JUVENILE NONFICTION / Social Topics / Death, Grief, Bereavement | JUVENILE NONFICTION /
    Social Topics / General (see also headings under Family)
Classification: LCC BF723.G75 L46 2023 (print) | LCC BF723.G75 (ebook) | DDC 155.9/37083—dc23/eng/20221017
LC record available at https://lccn.loc.gov/2022044369
LC ebook record available at https://lccn.loc.gov/2022044370

Edited by Cassie Sitzman
Cover and interior design by Courtenay Fletcher

Printed in China

Free Spirit Publishing
An imprint of Teacher Created Materials
9850 51st Avenue, Suite 100
Minneapolis, MN 55442
(612) 338-2068
help4kids@freespirit.com
freespirit.com

FSC
www.fsc.org
MIX
Paper from
responsible sources
FSC® C144853

For Noah, Ruthie Lou, and Maurice—K.L.

For Page, Bella, and Abe—M.M.

Someone I love died.

Did someone you love die too?
Who was it? What was their name?

After my special person died,
I had a lot of big feelings.

Sometimes I had all these feelings
at the same time.

I didn't know I could have so many
mixed-up feelings at once.

What did you feel after your
special person died?

When we love or care about someone and that person dies, we can feel grief.

We can feel grief for other reasons too.

We can feel grief when someone we love is
far away and we can't visit them.

We can feel grief when a pet dies,
when we move to a new home, or when
we change schools or teachers.

Grief is not just one thing.
It can be many.

Grief can be . . .

the mixed-up feelings we have after someone dies

missing the person

feeling sad

feeling lonely

being grumpy or
grouchy with people

feeling confused

FEELING ANGRY

I feel grief in
my body too.

My chest feels tight.

My hands feel hot.

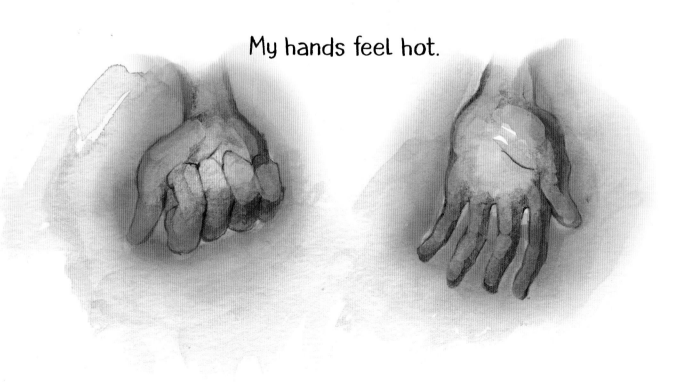

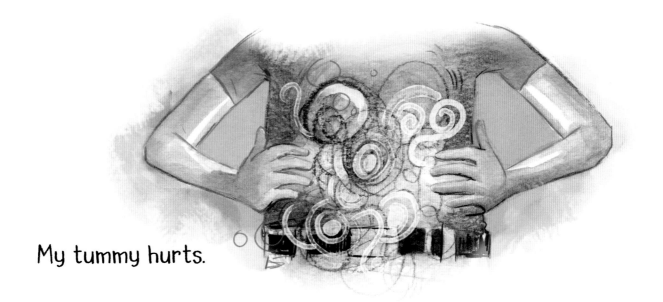

My tummy hurts.

My head feels foggy.

What does grief feel like in your body?

Sometimes grief feels like a color to me.

Grief can feel like one color, or it
can feel like lots of colors all at once.

If your grief were a color,
what color would it be?

Grief can feel BIG or small.

Is your grief big or small today?

Grief can be LOUD or quiet.

Is your grief loud
or quiet today?

When I feel grief, sometimes I want to be alone.

Other times, I want to be near my grown-ups.

Sometimes I want a hug, and other times I don't.

Do you want to be alone with your grief today, or near other people?

Some days, I don't feel my grief much at all.

Other days,
I feel my grief a lot.

It helps to talk with a
grown-up about it.

Who can you talk to
about your grief?

If I don't talk about my grief or
let grown-ups know how I feel,

ANGER fear

my grief can grow
BIGGER, and BIGGER, and BIGGER
on the inside.

When my grief grows too big, sometimes I do or say things that can hurt other people.

Sometimes I think sad or bad thoughts about myself.

What happens when your grief gets too big?

When my grief feels big and loud,
here are things I can do. I can . . .

talk about the
person who died,

draw or paint pictures
about them,

take deep breaths and
sometimes cry,

talk to a special grown-up
about my grief,

get a hug,
or hug a favorite toy.

What can you do when
your grief feels big?

Since the person we love died, everyone in my family feels grief. It helps when we share our grief.

We tell stories about the person who died,

look at photos of them,

make music or sing special songs that remind us of them,

go to a special place to remember them.

When someone special dies, people in my neighborhood and community feel grief too.

We have special ways to share our grief, like . . .

raising money in honor of the person who died,

lighting candles or lanterns,

putting flowers or other items in a special place.

What do you do in your family and community to help your grief?

Everyone feels grief sometimes.

Grief is a normal part of
missing someone special.

Grief can change
over time.

It might get
louder or quieter.

It may change color.
It could get bigger or smaller.

When grief feels big,
it can help to talk, play,
paint, and remember.

No matter what your grief is,
it's okay to feel it.

What does your grief feel like?

Helping Children Identify and Express Their Grief
A Guide for Caring Adults

If you are reading this book, it means that you are supporting a child experiencing the death of a loved one. It also means that you are likely navigating new terrain—a land of new language, new culture, and so many unknowns. If you are also grieving the loss of the person, you have the added challenge of carrying your grief *and* your child's.

So, as you set out through uncharted territory, remember to give yourself some grace. Supporting children through grief is not easy. You will make mistakes, and it will feel messy. You cannot do the grieving for them, nor can you make them grieve. *But you do not have to do this alone.*

There is no guidebook for how to support children through grief. However, there is *this* book to help you find the words, colors, shapes, and sizes to describe its complex and pervasive nature. In addition to the ideas and activities described in the story, the following pages provide typical responses children may have after the death of someone they love, examples you may relate to, activities and breathing exercises to help manage big emotions, and concrete and simple ways to help children express their grief.

Using the D Word

It's crucial when talking with children about death that you use the actual words. Yes, that means *death*, *dying*, and *dead*.

It's understandable to want to protect children and shield them from any more pain or discomfort. To this end, many people try to use the softer language of euphemism: "We lost them," "They're in a better place," or "They're living in heaven now." However, children hear these words through a very different lens.

A child's world is filled with fantasy and symbolism. The broom in your kitchen can turn into a rocket ship. A pile of sticks outside can transform into a unicorn squad or may become a heap of magic wands that grant wishes. Young children have the ability to believe that what they think and imagine can come true—even that bad things can happen to people they love because of something they said or did.

Heard through the ears of a child, euphemisms can evoke a sense of urgency, fear, and confusion. Here are a few examples of common euphemisms adults use to talk about death, and how they can confuse children.

- One four-year-old was told, "We lost your baby sister." This child then said matter-of-factly, "Well, let's go find her. Where did you lose her?" The child began to search around the house and continued this search for many months until the family sought support.

- Siblings aged three and five were told, "Daddy is in a better place." The siblings replied, "When can we visit him? Is he on one of his trips for work?"
- A five-year-old overheard a conversation between adults, "At least she's in heaven now, watching down on us." A week later, the family sought support after the child developed an intense fear of being alone. During a session, the child said, "I don't want grandma watching me when I'm in the bathroom."
- An eight-year-old was told, "The angels came to take mommy." Moments later, the child began to hyperventilate and burst into tears. He was inconsolable. When he could finally talk, he replied through sobs, "I don't want the angels to come and take me."

Be sure to provide a simple and concrete explanation of death: "When someone dies, their body stops working forever. They don't eat or drink. Their body doesn't sleep or play. Their heart stops beating, and they stop breathing forever."

During these conversations, watch and listen to children's cues. Turning away, losing interest, or beginning to play may be a child's way of telling you they've heard enough. When this happens, stop and return to the conversation at a later time. Often children will change the subject very quickly. For example, one four-year-old asked, "How did mommy die?" When provided a direct and simple answer, this child sat in silence for a moment, then said, "Can we get ice cream now?" Know that responses such as this are healthy and normal, and they don't mean that a child doesn't care or isn't grieving. They do mean that the child needs a break. This break may last hours, days, or even months or years, but eventually the child will be ready to revisit the conversation and add on a new layer of understanding.

You can follow up at another time, asking questions to identify misconceptions:

- "What do you think happens when someone dies?"
- "What do you think happens to a person's body when they die?"
- "Why do you think (insert the person's name) died?"

You may need to revisit these conversations with children many times, which can be hard if you are also grieving. But it is important to keep talking and answering their questions to help them understand the death.

How Children Respond to Grief

"If a child is old enough to love, they are old enough to grieve."—Alan Wolfelt

The following chart offers an age-by-age reference guide of common grief behaviors and reactions in children. Keep in mind that each child's grief is unique; no two children will experience it in the same way. The chart can help you recognize ways your child may be grieving, but it does not represent all the ways grief might manifest in children.

Age	Common Grief Behaviors & Reactions

Infants
(birth–12 months)

- fussiness and irritability
- feeding difficulties
- hard to soothe
- trouble with transitions and changing routines
- sleep and nighttime disturbances

Toddlers
(1–2 years)

- trouble with transitions and changing routines
- sleep and nighttime disturbances
- increased stranger-anxiety
- tantrums and outbursts

Pre-schoolers
(3–5 years)

- pauses in certain developmental milestones
- increase in fear (of the dark, monsters, other people)
- bad dreams or nightmares
- a desire to talk about the death—to anyone or everyone
- themes of death or loss in play
- increased need for physical closeness to caregivers
- statements about wanting to die or go to heaven (This is very common in young children who have been told about the death using euphemistic language.)

Early school-age children
(6–8 years)

- repeated questions about how the death happened, why it happened, where it happened
- preoccupation with body functions and what happens to a person's body when they die
- bursts and spurts of intense emotion
- difficulty concentrating
- trouble focusing in school or on any one thing at a time

Across all ages and developmental stages, grief can manifest in the body. It is common for children to have an increase in stomachaches and headaches and for their digestion to be impacted. Immune function may be activated, leading to more frequent colds and illnesses. Grief may also affect coordination—children and adults alike may be clumsier and fall more often. Fatigue and joint pain are other ways grief can show up in the body.

If your child is experiencing persistent symptoms or you have any concerns, it may be time to speak with a local grief counselor. Every hospice has bereavement counselors available, and every state in the United States has either a children's bereavement center or practitioners specializing in working with children who are grieving. You can search online to find contact information or check out the resources at the end of the book.

Common Grief Experiences in Children

In addition to common behaviors and reactions, young children may have common grief experiences. Keep the following in mind as you navigate grief with children.

As children grow and develop, so does their grief. A death occurring when a child is very young will be understood and revisited throughout their childhood and into adulthood. As children age, life milestones and special events may evoke a grief response. As a child's cognitive understanding matures, so too does their understanding of the death and their own grief. It is common for a child to begin asking more questions and wanting more complex information years after a death happens, even if you've already had such conversations.

Children grieve in spurts. One moment, they may be completely distraught and immersed in their grief, but in the next moment they ask for a snack or want to go play. This is normal. I like using the cup analogy to explain this experience: adults have a much larger cup to hold their grief, so their capacity to fill it before it overflows is larger. Children have a small cup—it overflows more quickly and easily.

Regressions in development can be expected. When children are young, they grow and change at a rapid pace. However, when stress occurs, it can interrupt their progress. I call this a pause. This might mean that children need help doing tasks they had previously accomplished independently, that a potty-trained toddler needs diapers for a time, or that a child who sleeps in their own bed needs to sleep with a caregiver. Though these developmental regressions are normal and expected, they can be alarming to adults. I encourage you to follow children's lead and remember that after a period (which could last days, weeks, or months), they will resume their developmental progress.

Children may include themes of death, dying, and loss in their play. While this may seem scary or alarming, know that it is normal and natural. Children process hard-to-understand experiences through play. Play enables them to make sense of, question, and explore complex topics. So after a death, it is common for children to play scenes of death too. They may play memorial service or funeral with stuffed animals, they may kill and bury toys, or they may play out themes of loss, such as losing a baby doll and having to find it or wanting to play hide-and-seek more often. Watching children play and playing with them can help you determine what they are struggling to understand and where they need more support.

New losses may remind children of prior losses. Whether it's a pet who dies or a celebrity, new deaths can propel children back into their grief experience. When these kinds of losses occur, it can be helpful to remind children that grief can happen when anyone or anything we care about dies. Use these moments as an opportunity to remember the loved one, together with the child.

Families grieve together, and apart. You know this better than anyone. Each member of a family has a unique and specific way that they manage and cope with stress. The same is true for grief. While the death of a loved one can alter the way a family functions as a unit, each person in that family is also individually grieving, on their own timeline and in their own way. Honor the differences in each person's grief.

Helping Children Express and Name Emotions of Grief

There is no right or wrong way to do these activities. Feel free to adjust them to suit children's needs.

Emotions Face Chart

An emotions chart can be a useful tool when helping children identify and express the many emotions that come with grief. You can download a free chart on this book's page at freespirit.com and use it at any time. Engaging in conversations about feelings is a healthy way for children to form strong emotional awareness skills.

Keep the chart in a place where children will see it frequently. Then, at various times throughout the day or week, use the chart to find the emotion you or the child is experiencing (even happiness). Ask "What does your grief look like today?"

Feeling Grief in the Body

Use this activity to help children recognize the way grief and related emotions feel in their bodies. Draw a simple human outline on a sheet of paper. Ask children the following questions and have them point out the body area on the human outline: *Where do you feel grief in your body? Where do you feel sad? Where do you feel angry? Where do you feel scared? Where do you feel lonely?* Invite children to color in the outline to artistically show how their grief feels.

When Grief Gets TOO BIG

Sometimes grief can feel overwhelming. In times when it feels like too much, the following activities can calm the body's nervous system and help children and adults settle their bodies and emotions. Before trying an activity, read through it and consider whether children are ready to participate in it as written. If not, adapt the activity or choose another one.

Box Breathing

Use your pointer finger and trace a square as you breathe. Breathe in for four counts as you trace the top of the square. Hold your breath for four as you trace down one side. Breathe out for four as you trace the bottom. And hold for four up the other side.

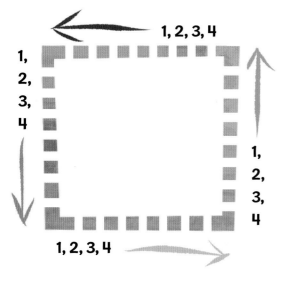

1, 2, 3, 4

1, 2, 3, 4

1, 2, 3, 4

1, 2, 3, 4

4-2-6 Breathing

Breathe in to the count of four. Hold for two. Then breathe out to the count of six. Repeat until you notice your body calming down.

Grief in a Jar

You will need an empty jar with a secure lid, loose glitter of various shapes and sizes, glitter glue, liquid soap, and food dye.

- Choose the colors of glitter that represent your grief.
- Fill the jar about three-quarters of the way with water and add in the glitter, a few drops of liquid soap, and a few squeezes of glitter glue. Use water to fill the jar all the way to the top.
- Secure the lid of the jar, shake, and add more glitter until you achieve the desired effect.

When grief is feeling too big, children can shake the jar and watch the glitter grief swirl. They can take big deep breaths and count how many it takes for all the glitter to settle. They may notice their grief settles too.

Anger Volcano

You will need a cookie sheet or another way to contain this messy activity (I often encourage families to do this activity outside if possible), an empty plastic bottle or cup, a measuring cup, a funnel, one tablespoon of baking soda, distilled white vinegar, and food coloring (if desired).

On the cookie sheet or outside, use the funnel to put the baking soda inside the bottle. You can also add a drop or two of food coloring if you want to relate the emotion in the volcano to a color.

Ask the child about a time when they felt a big emotion and they held their feelings inside instead of letting them out.

Add the vinegar to the bottle, using the funnel. You can do this slowly or quickly.

As the baking soda bubbles over, describe how this can happen when we hold our emotions inside and don't find ways to express what we feel. Talk about ways children can express their emotions and let them out.

Over my ten-plus years working with children grieving the death of a loved one, I have often used the questions in this book to help guide them in identifying and expressing their grief. A common question I ask is, *If your grief had a name, what would you call it?* A four-year-old sibling, whose baby brother died only weeks prior, once answered "I would call it The Big Sadness." This sibling's clear and descriptive response is one of the reasons I wrote this book. Young children and infants grieve just as deeply and painfully as adults do, yet they lack the experience necessary to process their grief. I hope this book provides a safe avenue for you to help the children in your life express, name, and make sense of their grief.

You know your child best. If at any point along their grief journey you are worried, please seek support from a local children's grief center or a therapist who specializes in children's grief.

Children's Grief Resources

The National Alliance for Children's Grief childrengrieve.org
The National Alliance for Children's Grief is a nonprofit organization that raises awareness about the needs of children and teens who are grieving a death and provides education and resources for anyone who supports them. They have a national directory of children's grief counselors, organizations, and camps organized by state.

Dougy Center dougy.org
A nonprofit organization dedicated to supporting grieving children and families. They have a physical location in Portland, Oregon, but they also have a wide range of free resources on their website.

About the Author and Illustrator

Dr. Korie Leigh is a certified child life specialist, certified thanatologist, and grief counselor. She specializes in child development and parenting and supporting children and families after a death. Dr. Leigh received her Ph.D. at the California Institute of Integral Studies, where she studied the experience of bereaved parents and siblings. She also has a bachelor's degree in child development from Wheelock College and a master's degree in public health with an emphasis in grief counseling from Brooklyn College. Dr. Leigh has practiced for over a decade as a child life specialist in children's hospitals and as a grief counselor in pediatric palliative care and hospice. Currently, Dr. Leigh is an associate professor and director of the Thanatology program at Marian University in Wisconsin and serves on the board of directors for Hero's Path Palliative, a pediatric palliative care organization. She has a private practice and enjoys spending time with her goofy dog Maisie and husband. Dr. Leigh lives in New Mexico.

Mike Malbrough is the illustrator of *You Made Me a Dad* and the Warren & Dragon chapter book series. He's the author-illustrator of *Marigold Bakes a Cake*, *Marigold Finds the Magic Words*, and *Love Is Here*, which received a starred review from *Kirkus*. During Mike's twenty-plus-year career, he has illustrated, designed, and/or built puppets, whales, robots, monsters, video games, hip-hop clothing, logos, retiring coworkers, and cute animals, but this winding road of doodling and artistry has at last landed him back home to where his journey began, telling stories for kids and families. Mike lives in northern New Jersey with his wife, two children, and his cat Agnes, who used to hate him but now won't leave him alone.